Your First Online Business

Contents

Introduction

Are you looking for a way to make more money, but don't want to go out and get another job? Would you like to learn how to increase your income by working online, straight from the comforts of your home, possibly without even getting out of your pajamas? If you answered yes to either (or both) of these questions, you are in the right place.

You probably already know that there are many ways to obtain what you want financially, because others have found them and profited from them tremendously already. You just need a little direction in your search. You need someone to tell you what options are available to you and how to get started with them and that is where this book comes in.

In it, you will learn ten different techniques to make money online (some of which contain several options within them). A few of them may take a while to learn and perfect, but others you can start using today, potentially earning you more income by the time the clock strikes midnight tonight.

What you are about to learn in the pages and chapters ahead is ten different techniques to make money with nothing more than an Internet connection and a will to get out of your current financial situation. While this list is certainly not all inclusive, it will give you an idea of the most popular Internet-based ways of making money available to you today.

In the end, it is up to you how profitable you are with any of these suggestions. You can make nothing or you can make a million dollars. Your ability to succeed is based on your ingenuity, creativity, ability to reach your target market, and unwavering perseverance. As long as you continue to learn from your mistakes, perfect your steps, and choose to do the best you can, then you will win in the end.

Chapter 1: Affiliate Marketing

The first, and perhaps most well-known online money making strategy is called affiliate marketing. It is the most important method of making money online, because you can combine it with almost any of the other methods that are in this book. Affiliate marketing involves selling other people's products or services on your website, social media page, YouTube account, and other Internet-based pages, thereby earning a commission on each sale.

Of course, this money making option requires that you have (or create) an Internet site or page and that site or page caters to the same market as the merchant or advertiser that you want to highlight and you should also have enough visitors. But once you have that, you could make some serious cash.

HOW TO GET STARTED

If the idea of affiliate marketing interests you, here is a quick step-by-step guide to getting you started:

Step #1: Select the category you wish to promote. This is pretty easy to do if you already have an existing site or page, as it is going to be one that is relevant to your subject or topic. For instance, if you currently own and operate a website that is somehow related to money or financial issues, you could increase your income base as an affiliate marketer (in which you would be called the publisher) by promoting and selling products and programs related to this topic (like the programs sold by Dave Ramsey, creator of Financial Peace University, or Jim Cramer, host of Mad Money).

However, if you don't have a page or site set up currently, what types of products or services are you interested in? What are some things that you are knowledgeable about and can discuss intelligently with your readers? Select a category that you love or could add value to and the rest of the process will be much easier for you.

Step #2: Set up a site or web page if you don't currently have one. If you don't already have a website or page set up, now is the time to do it. Some options to consider include developing a price comparison site, crafting a review site, or making a discount site for products that people commonly buy online as each one has the ability to attract consumers looking for specific items. Also, sites like these serve a functional purpose for the consumer; whether it is to help them save money, figure out which products are higher qualities, or both, while putting more money in your pocket at the same time.

Step #3: Decide what products or services you want to promote. If you don't believe in the product or service that you are an affiliate for, how can you expect your reader to be?

Think of the items that you have no problem recommending to your closest family and friends and your passion for them will shine through more clearly, getting your reader as excited about them as you are.

Step #4: Pick which affiliate marketing site(s) you'd like to use and set up an account. If you're new to affiliate marketing, you may want to check out sites such as Click bank, Amazon Affiliate Programs, E- Junkie, Pay Dotcom (which pays commissions via PayPal), and CJ Affiliate by Conversant (formerly known as Commission Junction). Each of these can direct you to the merchants best suited for you, allowing you to make the most money from your marketing affiliate program.

You'll want to pay close attention to how each one works and consider the impact it could have on your potential profits. For instance, Click bank lets you earn up to 75% of the product price and Pay Dotcom offers commissions up to 80%, but you may actually make more money off Amazon Affiliates even though they give you a lower percentage (6-15% depending on which program you choose) as they are one of the biggest online shopping retailers worldwide.

If you already have a successful blog or website that draws a lot of traffic, you may even get paid by a business for simply promoting their brand or name on your site, such as with Google Ad Sense. Options like this are often set up as pay-per-click, where you are reimbursed a certain rate for every person that clicks on the affiliate link that you have displayed somewhere on your site.

Step #5: How to select an affiliate program to promote. I will review the process on Click Bank because it is the website I recommend you to start with. First and most important is the commission you will get for each sale. Aim at 60%+ commissions for digital products. On average, most digital products on Click Bank sell between 35-85. Applying this rule you will be making at least 21$ per sale. If you promote physical products, don't stick with a specific percent but make sure you will earn at least 50$ per sale since physical products tend to sell harder than digital ones. Next make sure that the product has High Gravity. This means that a lot of people have made an affiliate sale in the past week, which basically means that the product is in high demand. However this will also mean that you have a lot of competition to sell the product. So my recommendation is to aim at products that have average gravity, but also have a great sales page. Make sure they have lengthy sales page and compare them with other competitive products, so you can see if they will covert well.

Step #6: Create a link to the specific product(s) that you'd like to promote and earn a commission from and attach it to your site. Once you have selected an affiliate program you want to promote, you should get an affiliate link. It is important that you just paste it on your website, blog or channel. If you place it on your website or blog, I recommend adding the link to the name of the program or something that represents it, instead of just pasting the link, which will be very unprofessional and also everyone will know that this is an affiliate link. If you are using YouTube to promote the product, you can use a link shortener like this one by Google "https://goo.gl." This way your links will look much more professional.

Step #7: Market your link. Now that your site is set up and ready to earn you some money, you must market your affiliate products as if they were your very own. Get your readers and followers interested in the items, programs, or services you have chosen so that they are willing to click on them and most importantly buy them.

Not only you want to promote these things on your base site, but don't be afraid to post about them (with the links) in groups or forums that are relevant to your target market too. The more exposure you can get, the higher your chance of making sales—and money.

Earning Potential

So, how much money can you make as an affiliate marketer? According to a poll conducted by Finch Sells, the majority of affiliates (just under 19 percent) earn $20,000 or less annually. Don't let that discourage you though. Almost six percent of the respondents reported that they earn over two million dollars a year by selling other people's products, services, and brands. That's worth it, right?

Therefore, it's largely up to you how far you will go and how much you stand to make with this particular online money making option. Obviously, the more traffic you can draw to your pages and the more time you put into promoting yourself and the affiliates that you've chosen to do business with, the more successful you will be.

If you want to increase your earning potential, it may benefit you to join an affiliate marketing forum like Digital Point, Warrior Forum, or a BestWeb. Forums such as these allow you to interact with other affiliate marketers who can provide you with the tips and tricks you need to help you succeed, thereby allowing you to earn a higher income at a faster rate than if you try to figure out affiliate marketing all on your own.

Chapter 2: YouTube

YouTube is the most popular video sharing website in the world, so I guess you are familiar with it to some extent. You can make money on it by creating your own channel and promoting either your own or other businesses' services and products, or you can participate in the YouTube Partner Program.

HOW TO GET STARTED

YouTube is much like any other social media site as far as set-up goes. But here are the steps you need to take to create a video channel worthy of hundreds, thousands, or even millions of viewers daily:

Step #1: Create your YouTube channel. Google has easy to follow, in-depth instructions that will help make the process of creating your own YouTube channel fairly simple. But first, you need to decide whether you want to set it up in your own name or the name of your business (if you have one). Think of what you want as your brand and choose the one that makes the most sense for you.

Also, another important factor to consider when creating your YouTube account is that you want to select keywords that your target market will likely use when they search for the products and services that you're selling so that you're more likely to show up in their results list. For instance, if your videos are about personal development, some good keywords include: raising self-esteem, feeling better about yourself, how to be self-confident, and developing a self-empowering attitude.

Once you get the logistics out of the way, you need to create an attractive YouTube channel. To do this, be sure to pick the right theme and color scheme for your topic area, and be sure to upload a picture that is representative of you or your brand so that your viewers can start to connect with you.

You must also select a video for your featured video on your YouTube channel, so make sure it is one of your best. Keep in mind that this may be what gets your target market to sign up for your posts (or leave your channel), so it needs to be one that entices them to do what you'd like.

Fill in the title and description using content that represents what you have to offer in a fun and interesting way. Any fields that you don't fill in should be removed so they don't clutter up your page, but be sure to leave the comment option intact on as this encourages your followers to connect with you, thereby raising your interaction, and your sales!

Step #2: Post videos. Once your YouTube channel is created, then you are ready to post your videos to it. What types of videos do best? Well, it depends on what you're trying to accomplish with them. Generally, shorter, high quality videos seem to get the most views. Therefore, it may be worth it to invest in good equipment and engage the help of friends so that you're not trying to do everything solo.

On the other hand, if you're demonstrating something or making a how-to video, it may need to be longer in length in order to convey a complete message. You want to get all of the necessary information in without talking fast or skipping over things in an effort to reduce your time.

To decide which will work best for your needs, think of what your target market would like to see and do your videos with those thoughts in mind. If you don't know, ask them and let them tell you what to direct next!

Step #3: Build your audience. As was mentioned in step one, selecting good keywords for your content helps drive traffic to your channel so keep that in mind when you're trying to target a select group of individuals. Use Google Keyword Planner to search for keywords based on your channel's niche. Make a list of the highest searched keywords. You should come up with about 20 here. List the keyword phrase along with the number of monthly searches. These are search keywords.

Next visit YouTube and make sure that you're logged out. We're going to be using the search function. Get the list that you just made and type the first three-four letters of the keyword phrase. YouTube will start listing suggestions as you type. This is no coincidence. These are keywords that other users are using to search for videos. You want to match these suggestions to the keywords in your list. These are your target audience's keywords.

And just as you should regularly post with other forms of social media, the same applies with YouTube. This will get more and more people to subscribe to your channel since they know that you will be uploading content consistently, making it easier to create a following.

Step #4: Cross-promote your videos. Share your videos on other forms of social media, such as Facebook and Twitter, to lead your followers and connections back to your YouTube site.

Encourage them to subscribe to your channel so they can easily see what you are going to do next. If you don't tell them to, they might not even think of it on their own. Get them excited about what you have to offer and make them want to be a part of it!

You can also start a website and/or blog and promote your videos there. I recommend that you use WordPress for the purpose, because it is free and very easy to set up. However I recommend that you invest 10$ in buying a domain name and also BUY a hosting for your website (you can use hostgator.com since they have really good prices). Free hosting is your worst enemy, never use it, because it will flood your website with random advertisement and it will look extremely unprofessional in the eyes of your audience.

Step #5: Set your YouTube account up to monetize with ads. You can take this step either right when you are uploading your video or after it is already live (although the first option is recommended so that you don't miss out on any cash). Do this by checking the "Monetize with Ads" option which can be found on the upload screen or by going to your Video Manager and doing it there after the fact.

Once your account is ready to be monetized, you'll also want to go to the Google AdSense website and create an account there. In order to do this, you need to be 18 years of age and have either a PayPal account or a bank account to get paid, so keep these parameters in mind before wasting your time by finding out that you don't have what you need.

Some ads are Cost per Click (CPC), which means that your advertiser pays when their ad is clicked on. Other ads are Cost per View (CPV), which requires that your viewer watch at least half of their ad, or 30 seconds worth, whichever comes first. Pre-roll ads are the ones that play prior to your video, while ads can also appear at the bottom of your video screen (called in-search ads) or on the side of it (in-display ads).

Each one has their own advantages, so it is really up to you which ones you want to use. You may even decide to try a couple of them and see which ones work best for your viewers. Change them around and see if it makes a difference for your income.

Step #6: Monetize your YouTube channel with affiliate marketing. Remember how the section on affiliate marketing said that you can make money on any Internet site? Well, YouTube is one of them, allowing you to direct your target market to the products and services that you feel will benefit them most by putting links on your YouTube page, making you money by selling other people's goods.

Again, you want to choose affiliates that would appeal to your target audience. So, choose the products and services most appropriate for your consumer so that you can make the most money possible.

You can also sell your own products and services on YouTube, earning 100 percent of the income, which is always a good thing.

Step #7: Check your stats and use the information wisely. YouTube provides you with analytics as to your video views so check them and see which ones are doing the best. Also, pay attention to which videos or topics aren't generating much buzz as that is equally as important to know.

The second part of this step involves using this information wisely. This means making changes to your strategy if something isn't working, but it also requires that you make more videos like the ones that are doing the best and capturing the most attention.

Step #8: Optional: Apply for a YouTube partnership. This particular step is only available to you after your YouTube channel has met certain criteria. Why apply for partnership? Because you have more content creation tools at your disposal and you can possibly win prizes based on the success of your channel. Either way, it is good for you.

Earning Potential

It is important to realize that you don't make money on YouTube based on the number of followers you have, but on how many of them engage with your ads and affiliates. Although they are definitely related, they are still independent of each other, which mean that you need to get your followers involved. It's not enough to just have them watch your videos.

One way to do this is to talk about your affiliates, ads, and products in your video. Give a call to action that tells your viewer to click on the links. If you don't, you may be wasting a good opportunity to increase your income.

So, how much money can you realistically make with YouTube videos? According to an article written by Business Insider, you can earn six figures with the right content, just like Olga Kay does, however it's likely going to cost you.

On the other hand you have many examples of twenty YouTube millionaires like Vitalyzd TV who has almost 8 million subscribers and make a fortune from his videos.

So is it worth it? Only you know the answer to that. It's possible that you may decide that this option may be best as a side job or you can device do dive in and do your best to make your star shine on YouTube, just go for whichever option you feel right at the moment.

Chapter 3: Blogging

A third way to make money online is by blogging. Blogging is defined as continuously writing about a situation, event, or other interest and posting it online for others to read. If you can create quite a following with your blog, you can also create a decent income.

HOW TO GET STARTED

To create a blog that draws major attention and begin to draw money from it, here's what you need to do:

Step #1: Decide what you want your blog to be about. What topic or topics interest you most? Are you a car geek who knows everything and anything about the cars and trucks on the road today, or do you have an insatiable appetite for cooking and want to share your passion with others who feel the same?

Some of the most profitable niches and blog ideas are tech review blogs, beauty and fashion, health and nutrition, how to make money, or even teaching people how to blog! However, it is very important to only blog about things that you are genuinely interested in. Otherwise, you won't be able to engage other people in the topic if you have no interest in it yourself.

Once you have a list of options, pick a topic and tailor it down as specifically as you can to better resonate with your target market. For instance, if you enjoy cooking, what style speaks to you most? Are you a farm-to-table chef or do you like making traditional foods with a modern flair? The more specific you can make your topic, the easier it will be to reach the people you intend to reach.

To look for inspiration with this, check out related blogs that others are writing. This may help you come up with ideas for your own, in addition to helping you see what parts of their blog you like, and which ones you don't, making your blog easier for you to create, which is the next step.

Step #2: Create your blog. If you already have a blog in place, you are one step ahead of the game. If not, then you need to create one. You can do this by putting a blog page on your own website, or by joining a pre-existing blog platform, such as WordPress, that has easy-to-use themes that make setting up your blog a cinch.

Your number one priority is to come up with a domain name that suits you and is easy for your followers to remember and recognize. Something short and catchy will often do the trick, like 3 Fat Chicks who offer weight loss support or Dumb Little Man who provides tips about life. Also, don't try get too close to a well-known trademarked name in an attempt to get more followers or you could run into problems.

If you are setting up your blog on a self-hosting website such as Hostgator, Bluehost, or Dreamhost, all of which have packages for less than $10 per month, remember that .com's often work the best as that is what most people are used to. At this point, .net is becoming more universal as well, so that is an option you may want to consider.

You also want to create a page that is pleasing to your target market and consistent with your brand. Choose colors and graphics that are representative of your style and topic, making it easy for your potential client base to tell who and what you are about at a glance.

Step #3: Start posting. The key to effective blogging is to create articles that your target market would want to read that contain keywords so you are easier to find. This involves creating a title that draws them in and writing a blog that engages interests, entertains, and benefits them in some way, while still making sure that each part of your blog has the keywords where they need to be. Also always format your articles to look appealing and to be easier to read.

You can either write these on your own or hire a ghostwriter to write them for you. If you choose a ghostwriter, one great platform to hire from is Elance. Each freelance writer is rated based on their past performance with previous clients, allowing you to pick the one that is best for you after reviewing their profile and job proposal on your specific project.

Don't be afraid to post videos or pictures on your blog either. People resonate with different types of material, so mix your blog up to suit most every type of reader or viewer and you'll have a larger impact, as well as a larger following.

One very important thing to remember is to post regularly. Get your readers used to seeing your name so they feel like you're a trusted friend and make them look forward to your posts, as if you are a part of their everyday life.

Some people choose to post on a specific schedule, like every Saturday morning at 8:00 AM. However, others post randomly and only when they have something to say. Find what works best for you and stick to it. I recommend that in the beginning you post as much as possible, without sacrificing quality of course. Aim at 2-3 times a week in order to build a larger following on your blog.

Step #4: Build your following by promoting your blog. Once you have some posts on your blog, now is a good time to promote it to build your following. First and foremost, you want to add the right keywords to your blog and the posts it contains so that your target market can easily find you when they do a search.

Second, you want to encourage them to follow your blog by offering a free download upon signing up, building your followers quicker and more effectively. Put a "Subscribe" button on it so that they can easily sign up to receive your posts as you make them (I recommend using AWeber.com or mailchimp.com for this purpose). Ask them to share them with their family and friends, who can then subscribe as well.

Step #5: Monetize your blog. Implementing what you've already learned about making money online in Chapter 1, your blog is a great place for affiliate marketing and CPC (Cost Per Click) ad networks like Google AdSense. Both of these options can draw in some good money if you have a huge following on your blog.

CPM ad networks will also pay you for reaching your viewers. The rate is measured per 1,000, so the more followers you have, the more money you stand to make. Some options, if this is a route you choose to take, are AdClickMedia, Twelvefold Media, and SiteScout.

Additionally, you can sell your own products and services on your blog too and monetize it that way. If you're a freelance writer, for instance, you can offer your followers content packages for their business (such as for their web page, emails, or their blog), or if you are a motivational speaker, you can offer to talk to organizations and groups to inspire them to reach higher levels and achieve higher goals.

You could also create your own e-book (which we'll go over in Chapter 8 of this book) and sell it on your blog for some residual income that could really add up over time. Be creative with monetizing your blog and think of the endless possibilities when it comes to making money on it.

Step #6: Promote your blog. Promote your blog on other platforms (such as your web page, social media accounts like Facebook and Twitter, YouTube, etc.) to draw others to it. Follow and post on other people's blogs, inspiring their curiosity to go to your blog and check out what it is about. Since you already have content on your blog posting the same content as a video on YouTube, is an easy way to reach more people and invite them to your blog, and also a lot of people these days prefer to watch videos, rather than reading articles.

Another option is to allow guest posting on your blog, making others to want to be a part of it. This also helps them share your blog as well, as it benefits them to get their name out while getting yours out at the same time.

Join LinkedIn groups about and for bloggers and any other blogging groups you can find. When people ask questions within these groups about your topic, write a blog about it and refer them to it. It's a great way to establish you as an expert in the field, making them more likely to buy the products and services you recommend.

Earning Potential

Here's the big question: How much can you earn by blogging? Well, depending on how big you grow your blog and how you choose to monetize it, you can make over $2 million per month, like the Huffington Post whose main income is in pay per click ads. Or you could make a lot less, such as Expert Photography who draws in roughly $5,000 per month via affiliate sales.

Some blogs don't make anything because they don't entice their reader to want to take action. Remember that while you're having fun with your blog, you're not going to make any money with it if you don't ask your readers to buy your products, purchase your affiliate's products, or click on the ads.

Find what works best for you and what connects most with your target market and you're on your way to creating a blog that brings in more in a month than some people make in a year. Who knows? Your blog may just be the next one to go viral, earning you a great annual income that will give you a nice, comfy life, long into retirement.

Chapter 4: Fiverr

Fiverr is a website that allows you to sell your talent or talents for an income. For instance, are you a creative writer, SEO guru, design artist, website creator, or do you have talent as a voice-over artist? Then you can make money as a seller on Fiverr by providing your unique and talent-driven services to people and businesses whoever needs them.

How to Get Started

To make money on Fiverr, just take these steps:

Step #1: Decide what you want to sell. What products or services can you offer others relatively quickly and for a low starting amount (think $5 per gig)? Ideally, you want to come up with something unique so that you have less competition, but any skill that you have can easily be sold on Fiverr as there are lots of buyers available.

Step #2: Sign up for an account. You can create a Fiverr account using your email address, Google+ account or Facebook to sign in. You just have to confirm it and then you are good to go.

Step #3: Set up your profile. Once your account is created, you want to set up your profile, which means uploading a picture and telling Fiverr a little bit about who you are.

The consistent theme across this platform seems to be that less is better. So, you're going to want to be as clear and concise as you can in order to fit all of your content in. Be straight and to the point or you're going to be cut short. Also make sure that you use a professional looking photo for your profile picture (or your logo), you don't want to scare away potential buyers.

Step #4: Verify your idea. But before you start creating your first gig, make sure that your idea is worthwhile. Go on fiverr and search for similar gigs. Make sure that there is a demand for similar services like yours. Type your keywords and see if you can find at least 3 gigs that have more than 500 reviews and more than 10 orders in queue. If you find them, then good, this means that your idea is in high demand and you can make real money with it. Now let's proceed with creating your gig.

Step #5: Create a gig. Click on "Start Selling" under your profile and create a gig, which is another name for the service or product you want to sell. We will break this step into smaller steps that need to be taken in order to build a bestselling gig.

So let's start with your gig title. You only have 80 characters for your gig title, so use them wisely. Fiverr even tells you that short titles sell more, so heed their advice, also it is very important that your title clearly describes what you offer; don't use confusing titles, because this will bring you a lot of angry buyers.

Next you want to have a very appealing and competitive gig samples. Again make sure to take a look around Fiverr in order to see how people represent their gigs. Use this for inspiration and also for a reference how good your gig should look. If you can make it look better and more appealing than the other gigs that are already available, then great. If you are not a graphic designer consider hiring one from fiverr who can create you cool images to represent your gig.

After you are done with your samples you should continue with the gig description. Make sure that you use the formatting options that fiverr offers, so it can be easy to read and highlight all the key points. Explain your service in detail, what you offer for 5$ and what you offer as an extra. Look at your description as a contract with the client that defines your service.

Next it is recommended that you upload a video. Gigs that have a video tend to gain popularity more easily, because they get a better placement in the search results when they are published. You can simply record yourself explaining your service, also don't forget to mention the phrase "this gig is exclusively on fiverr.com", and make sure that your video looks professional and you don't have your bed in the background or something embarrassing.

Step #6: Promote your gig. Fiverr makes this step super easy as well as once you have all of the information they are requesting, you can publish your gig via social media buttons before even leaving the page. They have one for Facebook, Twitter, Google+, LinkedIn, or via email. All you have to do is click the one you want and they will tell the rest of the world (or your followers anyway) about your brand new service offering! Also make sure to optimize the keywords for your gig. It is better that they match the title of your gig, because this way they will have greater impact. Just like I recommended in the "YouTube" section use the Google Keyword Planner to determine the best keywords for your gig.

Step #7: Provide GREAT customer service. Because Fiverr allows the buyers to rate you, you're going to want to be a true professional to them so that you get a higher score. Of course, you can't always please everyone, but the happier your clients are overall, the more work you'll get and the more money you'll make. There is a golden rule to Fiverr long term success "Just over deliver". Make sure that you surpass your buyer's expectations. You can do so by applying a simple trick. For example if you are a writer and you want to offer to write articles, the usual word count for 5$ is between 300-500 words. If you are ok writing 500 words for 5$, you can offer in your gig 400 words for 5$, but always deliver around 500. This way the clients will be very pleased with your service and will come back.

Sometimes you will meet some bad buyers of course. Then you have to put your long term interests over and above your short term losses. They will be more demanding and pays less. Let a bad client go professionally and respectfully and focus on your good clients instead. Also never try to please a bad client, because you don't want a bad returning client.

Step #8: Learn from other Fiverr sellers. One of the best ways to learn is to mirror what others are doing on Fiverr that seems to be working for them. Dion appears to be one of the top sellers, so you might want to check him out and see what he can teach you about what it takes to be a top seller like him!

Earning Potential

You must start out at $5 per gig, be on the site at least 30 days, and complete a minimum of ten orders in order to start making real money on Fiverr. But if you are fast at what you do, you can earn a decent amount of spending cash off this particular site as long as you're comfortable working on a number of different projects in order to do so.

Some Fiverr members have reported earning hundreds of dollars a day, which is possible as long as you get a lot of gigs as a top seller or are able to sell add-ons. I make around 2,000$ a month from Fiverr with for about 50 hours a month. This requires quite a time commitment to achieve, but it is possible if you're good at whatever it is you are selling and can get a lot of buyers to want your services.

Chapter 5: Selling Physical Products Online

Another way to earn money online is by selling physical products on sites like Amazon and eBay. While you may not earn enough to make a living selling your own personal items (unless you are able to acquire a lot of goods at low costs and can turn them around quickly), you can also help others sell their things, thereby earning yourself a nice little commission in the process.

HOW TO GET STARTED

How do you get started selling? Here are a few simple steps:

Step #1: Find a product to sell. Your first step to making this Internet option work is finding a product to sell. Fortunately, there are several ways to go about it. For instance, you can start by taking a look around your house and seeing what you have that you no longer want or need as selling your unwanted or unused items is a great way to get them out of your house without just sending them to the trash. The key to making a lot of money is to make sure they are still in good, if not excellent condition.

That being said, some people do sell broken things online as others may be buying them with the intent of fixing them and offering them for resale. So, in essence, nothing is off limits ("one man's junk is another man's treasure") as long as you are honest and market it accordingly.

A second option is to frequent yard and garage sales (and swap meets, flea markets, and antique sales), as sometimes you can find great deals there that you can resell online. Whether the item you purchased is in great condition already or you have what it takes to refinish it, you can make a lot of money off other people's no longer wanted goods.

If you can find a really good deal at retail or even wholesale stores, you can also buy direct from them and resell the items at a higher price. Liquidation events, going out of business sales, and discontinued items are great for this purpose. Just be aware that buying items with the sole purpose of resale may require that you pay tax on them, so you may want to consult with an accountant before taking that route.

Good items to consider selling are ones that appeal to a niche market. Hobbyists like to find unique things online, making this one area that you can do really well in.

Still not sure what to sell? EBay has a Selling Inspiration House that can help you "find top-selling items in your home." Just pick a room, select an item, and it will tell you how much they are currently going for online.

Step #2: Pick a platform and create an account. Now that you have something to sell, it is time to decide where it is you want to sell it. Two of the most notable sites are Amazon and eBay. However, you can also list your item on Craigslist (best for bigger items like cars and furniture).

Be sure to read each one carefully so you know up front what is required of you as a seller and how much commission they will take on the sale. Some charge you to a subscription fee as well, so you're going to want to check all of this out prior to signing up.

Whichever one you choose, you're going to have to create an account in order to list and get paid. So, pick the one (or ones) that is best suited for you and the items you want to get rid of, and provide all of the requested information to create a complete account.

In order to get your money from them, you are also going to have to provide payment information. To keep your bank information private, you can always create a PayPal account and accept payment that way. (PayPal does charge fees as well, so you may have to weigh that into the cost and whether or not it is worth it given what you are selling.)

A great way to figure out which site you prefer is to buy something from it before even placing your goods for sale. This way you get firsthand knowledge of how it works from the buyer's perspective, allowing you to take them into consideration when it comes to selling your goods online.

Step #3: Prepare your listing for optimal results. To get good results on your listing, you want to include both benefits and features of your product. For example, features of a TV include screen size, resolution, and things like that, whereas benefits are being able to see the television clearer, having a flat- screen that doesn't take up too much room, and being able to see your favorite sports up close, almost as if you were there in person.

Your product description needs to be complete as well. The more information you provide about what it is you're selling, the easier it will be for people to determine if that is what they are looking for. Think like a buyer and include everything you would want to know if you were making the purchase yourself.

It helps to be familiar with jargon that is often used on popular selling sites. For example, BN stands for brand new and VTG means vintage. HTF represents a hard to find item and VGC tells the buyer it is in very good condition. If something is unique or distinct about your product, point it out. The more you can make your product a "one of a kind," the greater your chance of selling it.

Use keywords in your listing so that your product can be easily found by anyone searching for it. Not sure which ones to use? Consider what words you would use to search for the item and just use them. Include the brand if it is likely to make a difference.

Your product pictures (the more the better) need to be high quality. If they are fuzzy or too far away, you're not going to give prospective buyers a good feeling. Also, make sure the surrounding environment is good too because people like to buy from others who appear to take care of their things.

If you're stuck on any of these things, look up other people's listings and use them as templates to write yours. Just be sure to choose a top seller so that you know how to create an ad that sells, not one that doesn't get noticed.

Step #4: Set your price. As far as price is concerned, this one may take a little bit of research. Google the item you are selling and see what others are getting for it. Before pricing yours though, you'll want to take into consideration its condition.

Depending on the site you intend to use, you can sell your item via traditional auction or by set price. Auction means that you sell to the highest bidder (and you may want to set a minimum price so you don't practically give it away) and set price means that you sell it to anyone that wants it for the price which you are selling it.

If you have a bunch of smaller items and don't want to price them for individual sale, you may want to group them together and sell them as a package. This may also entice a buyer as they will be getting several things for one standard rate.

An additional tip: some successful sellers offer free shipping as it catches people's attention. It's easy enough do as you just have to add this amount to your base price. The one caveat is that shipping isn't always going to be the same price as it is location dependent. So, you're going to want to keep this in mind if you choose to take this route.

Step #5: List your product on Amazon or eBay. When you decide to list your product, you'll want to time your listing so you get the most out of it. For example, if you only have a 10-day window, you may want to post your product on a Thursday so that it appears online for two full weekends, giving you more bangs for your buck.

Another factor to consider is whether your item is seasonal, or in high demand during certain times of the year. If this is the case, you may want to wait to sell it, drawing in the most money possible.

Step #6: Promote your product. Share your product on your social media sites, website, in forums, or on any other Internet site you can think of to draw attention to it. You never know. Even if the people you're reaching out to have no interest in it, they might know someone who does and share it with them. It's a win-win!

Step #7: Make the deal. Once you have a specific buyer, you're ready to close the deal. This is a great time to confirm things such as price and delivery, as well as answer any questions they may have.

This is also where you collect payment. It is very important that you do this prior to shipping your item so that you don't wind up sending it out and never getting the money, in return.

Step #8: Deliver your product. You want to make sure your item arrives in the same condition it left you in, so you're going to want to pack it well. Do this by putting in extra padding to avoid unintentional breakage or damage by the shipping company. You can even go one step further and take pictures of your item as it is being packaged as well as the finished box to show what condition it was in when it left you.

Then ship it according to the site's requirements, being sure to get a tracking number and insurance if you want to be extra safe or the item is worth a lot of money. Having your buyer sign for it ensures that they received it, and it protects you from scammers who insist that it never arrived.

Step #9: Grow your product-based business. In order to survive long-term and grow on sites like eBay, you need to get good feedback from the people that you sell to. Keep this in mind as every interaction you have with your customers has the potential to promote your business—or break it.

Staying in good contact with them every step of the way will help establish a good buyer/seller relationship. Check your email often and don't list things while you're going to be away for an extended period of time as it could look bad on you as a seller.

Conclusion

Making money online is possible and you now have the viable options from which to choose. Try one or try them all and see which one suits you, your home life, and your desired outcome best.

These can be your hobbies which can produce incomes capable of supporting you and your family easily (such as mobile apps and SEO). But none of them will work unless you put the time and effort into them that they require.

There is no such thing as easy money; there is only becoming more efficient and effective so that it comes to you faster and with less effort. Hopefully now it will.

Now get out there and make some money with nothing more than your internet connection!